HOW TO REPAIR THE EXTERIOR OF YOUR HOME

HOW TO REPAIR THE EXTERIOR OF YOUR HOME

Jackson Hand

THEODORE AUDEL & CO.
a division of
HOWARD W. SAMS & CO., INC.
4300 West 62nd Street
Indianapolis, Indiana 46268

ISBN: 0-672-23816-0

Manufactured in the United States of America

Produced by Ottenheimer Publishers, Inc.

CONTENTS

1

DOORS AND LOCKS

SINCE DOORS AND WINDOWS *operate*—open, close, lock, switch from wintertime to summertime function, etc.—they present more frequent repair problems than any other component of the house structure. They are the only elements of a house with moving parts that can go bad. They are always subject to traffic and manipulation. Add to that the fact that most of the time a fragile material, glass, is involved.

Fortunately, everything about doors is simple, with the exception of "locksmithing," and can be taken care of with tools around the house. The only requirement is an understanding of the troubles that may arise and of the principles that make doors and windows work smoothly.

THE STICKING DOOR

A door is a fairly big piece of wood, subject to a great deal of swelling and shrinking with changes in humidity. That is the reason why many doors are made in panel form; the individual panels shrink and swell in their own frames without changing greatly the overall size of the door. Shrinkage is also low with most modern flush doors that are of laminated, plywood-like construction over special "cores" that don't react much, if at all, to moisture changes.

With either type of door, however, there is almost always enough dimensional change with weather changes to cause binding at least once. That is, the carpenter hung the door and it worked. However, when the maximum humidity season came along, the door swelled enough to make trouble. Normally, you fix it once, and that's it.

Naturally, it's best to work on the door at a time when it is at its biggest. Your objective should be the closest tolerable fit when the door is at its largest. Do not commit the error of overdoing it, making the door too loose when it is swollen to full dimension, or it may be entirely too small at the other end of the cycle.

Fitting a door without planing. In the majority of cases you can cure the problem instead by manipulating the hinges. It is a little known fact that you can move the "strike edge" of a door toward or away from the frame, and you can tilt that edge up or down through the use of cardboard shims or spaces inserted back of the hinges. To do this, you loosen the hinge screws two or three turns. They are still gripping the wood, so the door doesn't fall, but the hinge flange comes free from the wood. Ordinarily, you will not use enough shimming back of the flange to affect the grip of the screws. However, if you feel they might not be doing their job when you retighten them, remove one screw at a time, stick a couple of pieces of toothpick in the hole, and redrive the screw.

The kind of shim and the specific place where you insert it determine which direction the door takes. The possibilities, illustrated in the accompanying photographs and drawing, are based on shifting the position of the hinge barrel, where the pin is, and thus shifting the position of the entire door.

If a door sticks *at the strike edge*, it must be moved away from the jamb toward the hinge edge. Do this by inserting a strip of cardboard between the hinge flange and the jamb, at the edge of the hinge opposite the barrel, position A on the drawing. This pivots the hinge around the edge of the jamb, moving the barrel slightly away from the edge where it is sticking.

If a door binds *at the hinge edge*, that is, comes up snug against the jamb before it is fully closed, you can loosen that snugness by putting the strip of cardboard between the hinge and the jamb at the side of the hinge toward the barrel position B on the drawing. When you do this, you move the barrel away from the jamb, carrying the door with it.

If a door sticks *at the top corner*, you can tilt the entire door by putting *two thicknesses* of cardboard back of the entire hinge at the top, *one thickness* at the middle hinge if there is one, and none at the bottom hinge.

If the door sticks *at the sill*, reverse the procedure, putting two shims at the bottom and none at the top.

All of these corrections assume that there is, indeed, room for the door to move in the direction it must go to eliminate the problem. If there is no room, if the door is simply too big for the opening, there is no choice except to plane it down. However, try the hinge manipulation technique first; it has the tremendous advantage of producing no raw wood that must be given a finish to make it match the rest of the door.

HINGE MANIPULATION SOLVES
MANY STICKING DOOR PROBLEMS

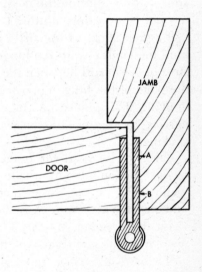

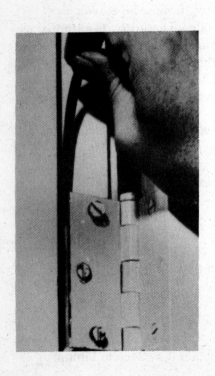

With the screws loosened, slip a piece of cardboard in back of the hinges on the edge away from the barrel (at A in drawing), to move a door away from the strike side.

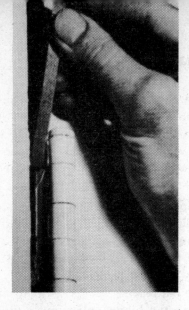

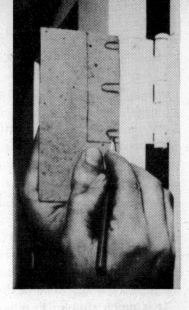

Conversely, put the piece of cardboard back of the hinge on the side toward the barrel (at *B* in drawings), to move the door closer to the strike.

To tilt a door, releasing binding at an upper or lower corner, cut shims to fit back of the hinges. Mark the positions of the screws first.

Slip the shims back of the hinges, using two at the top, one in the middle if there are three hinges, and none on the bottom. Or reverse this to tilt the door up. Use shims back of all hinges equally to move the door toward the strike.

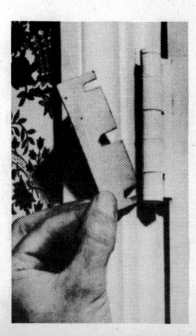

Planing a door to make it fit. It is usually best to do the planing on the hinge edge. You can take off a few shavings on the strike side if only a small amount of planing is necessary, and you may be able to do it without demounting the door. However, if a considerable amount of wood must be removed, *take the door down.* And do all the planing on the hinge edge.

The reasons for this are important. First, that is the least conspicuous edge, in case you find it difficult to finish the planed areas to match. More important, however, is the problem of planing in the area of the door lock. It must be removed. In severe cases it may even be necessary to modify the holes, actually to *move* the hardware.

It is much simpler to remove the hinges, plane away the required amount of wood, then if necessary cut the hinge mortises a little deeper.

To move a door away from the strike side, cut the hinge mortises deeper on the jamb or the door, or both.

Taking a door down. Remove the hinge pins first (see photo). Take out the pin of the bottom hinge first and the top pin last. That way, the door won't fall over, possibly tearing a lower hinge loose doing other damage. Some hinges have a decorative ball on the bottom of the barrel, to match the knob on the pin. When that is the case, check to see if there is a small hole in the bottom, into which you can insert a nail to drive the pin up. If not, you may have to work a screwdriver into the crack beneath the shoulder of the pin to raise it.

Then with the door down, take out the screws that hold the hinges on. (In rare cases, there may be no hinge pin and you'll have to remove the hinges screws to take the door down.)

If the weather stripping system used in your home has metal

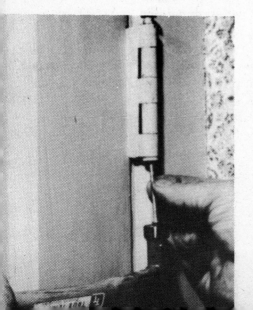

When you must take a door down, to plane it for example, the easy way is to remove the pin. In some cases you may have to drive it up with a nail through a hole in the bottom.

parts fastened to the door itself, you will have to remove them in order to do any essential planing. However, the weather-stripped door does not often stick, since the stripping is flexible and occupies enough space to allow for a considerable expansion.

Lubrication. This may lick a sticking door, without any need for planing or hinge manipulation. If the problem is slight, try a little candle wax or "lube stick" at the point where the door sticks. Or, pick up a can of spray lubricant, usually a silicone formula, and treat both the jamb and the door edge. These spray materials usually dry invisibly, and they may cut down friction enough to get you through the high humidity season, until the door starts to shrink again, and the problem disappears.

If a door is too small. It takes tremendous humidity extremes plus some poor handymanship to turn up a door that is too small, that was planed too much when it was installed, or too much at the point of its widest dimension. But it can happen. To rectify the situation, you must add size to the door.

The best place to do it is on the hinge edge. Cut a piece of wood the right thickness to provide the required width and glue it to the edge. Cut pieces to fit the hinge mortises and glue them in place. You will probably find it necessary to put matchstick-size pieces of wood in the screw holes, since the screws will not go as far into the holes as they did originally.

In some cases, on access doors, it may be possible to increase the effective size of a door by installing a type of weather stripping that fills the space more completely.

WHAT TO DO WHEN A DOOR RATTLES

When a door is properly hung and fitted, it closes against the stop and the door catch springs into the strike, and there is no free space. When this rather critical fit is too loose, the door can rattle back and forth between stop and catch. There are several ways to stop the rattling, some of them more suited to inside doors, some to outside doors.

Felt cushion. Once or more thickness of felt, cemented to the stop in the upper corner, will often "squeeze" the door tightly enough between stop and strike to end rattle. This is most likely to work successfully on bedroom and other inside doors.

Weather stripping. If weather stripping deteriorates or compacts over a period of time, it no longer exerts its gentle pressure against the door. You may be able to move the stripping closer, or you may find it necessary to replace it with new material.

Mechanical changes. For the best job, and the only one, in severe cases, you must move the strike on the door jamb, remounting it closer to the strike. Begin by observing the *amount of adjustment* necessary. With the door pushed hard against the strike, scribe a knife-blade mark on the jamb at the edge of the door. Now pull the door hard against the strike and make another mark. The distance between these marks is the distance the strike must be moved. Actually, you'll want to move it a hair more than that—see below.

Remove the strike and fill its mortises with a close-fitting patch of wood, glued in place. When the patch is dry, cut the new mortise in the proper new position and screw the strike on. If your measurements and your mechanics were accurate, the door should now latch when it is closed firmly against the stop. However, if the door is closed gently, it may not catch.

Try this trick. File a gentle bevel on the flat side of the bolt, so that it will catch even if the door is closed slowly. Then, the spring will hold the latch in and any of the sort of vibration that would have caused door rattling will merely result in deeper seating of the catch.

The door doesn't latch. Although it doesn't happen often, there are times when swelling and shrinking of the wooden parts of a door and jamb, settling of the house, or warping may cause a situation in which the spring-driven latch doesn't snap into the strike plate opening when the door is closed. Not even when it is banged shut. It is usually easiest to fix this by removing the strike plate and filing a little metal off the square bolt in the strike, to let the latch pop into place. However, you must first determine where to file. It may be that the latch is catching on the front, or the top, or the bottom. You may be able to determine which by careful examination; you can usually see if it is catching above or below by squinting into the crack when the door is closed. If it seems to be neither, then you can figure that it is the front edge. (It can be both the front *and* the top or bottom, of course.) Put the strike in a vise and do the required amount of filing. Combine this, perhaps, with the latch-bevel filing mentioned above. The two operations should make it unnecessary to move the strike, a much more difficult job.

The door doesn't bolt. If your lock has a "dead bolt," that is, a square, rugged bolt that you must throw by turning a knob or key, it is possible for it to go out of alignment and miss the hole intended for it in the strike plate. Use the filing technique covered above to correct this problem. Do not, however, file the bolt itself.

PROBLEMS WITH THE DOOR LOCK MECHANISM

If the locks on your doors are typical they are likely to have bright and shiny knobs on the outside, but they may have fairly unreliable mechanisms on the inside. Not only does this make them subject to breakdown, but to breakin. In many cases, at the first sign of mechanical deficiency, your best move is to replace the entire lock with one that is equal to its responsibilities, in home security.

The most common problems with locks are these.

Loose handle or knob. Sometimes they're even so loose that they come off. On most locks, the handle or knob slips on a square shaft or screws on a square shaft with threads. It is held in place by a set screw, usually located at the slimmest part of the knob. Because of the constant open-close action, this set screw loosens and so does the knob. To fix it, loosen the screw. Slip or twist the knob up snug, then tighten the screw. With the threaded square rod, you may tighten things a half-turn or so too much. This will keep the knob from snapping back into "neutral," when you let go of it. If this happens, untwist the knob a quarter turn, then set the screw.

You may discover—it happens often—that this problem recurs, because the situation that causes it, traffic, continues. If so, get hold of a small tube of material that locks threads, sold by hardware stores. Or use a dab of silicone calk over the end of the set screw, to keep it from loosening with repeated movement.

This is a typical simple lock. To remove it, loosen a screw on one of the knobs and slip it off. Then, remove two screws through the flange into the door. This lets the two halves of the lock come free. The latch then comes out of its hole in the edge of the door. Some locks may be designed so the knob doesn't have to be removed; you can loosen screws by working around it.

Handles that stick. Gradual infection of the mechanism by moisture-laden air that eventually gums up the operation usually causes sticking handles. If the problem is mild, you can take care of it with "graphite lube" injectors hardware stores sell, or with spray lubricants. Turn the handle to retract the catch. Spray through the opening. Let the handle return to its normal position. Open it again, and again spray or inject.

If a few rotations of this procedure do not free the sticki-ness, you may have to remove the lock from the door and give it a thorough cleaning and oiling. This is not difficult with the average lock, and the following steps can be adapted to handle most circumstances:

Unscrew the set screw and remove the inside knob. Now the "twisting mechanism" of the entire lock should pull out, on the inside. Next remove the screws in the edge of the door holding the lock in place. You should be able to pull the latch mechanism out. The accompanying photograph is typical of the most common type of locks. If you will put it together in the open, as shown, it will help you to understand the mech-anism from now on.

To restore this lock to excellent working condition, you should dunk it in a solvent (kerosene, gasoline, paint thinner) to clean away old, thickened lubricants and any accumulation of dirt and grease. Then daub it with three-in-one oil, or equivalent, to make all springs, slides and turns free acting.

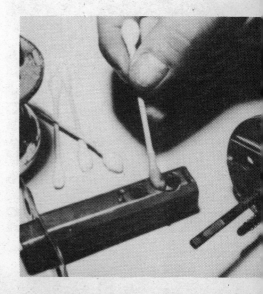

Although a lock can usually be lubricated by spray graph-ite or other lubricants, it is sometimes necessary to dis-mantle the entire setup and swab the working parts with light oil.

Catches that stick. Usually victims of the same situations as stuck handles, they are, fortunately, more easily licked by spray or injected lubrication. Spray in the opening, then jab the catch in repeatedly with repeated spraying, until the mechanism works smoothly.

REPLACING A LOCK

Even if the locks on your access doors are not giving you any trouble, it may be that you should replace them, as a means of giving trouble to other, unwelcome people. It is a fact that the typical lock on the typical door is not much of a barrier to the typical breaker-and-enterer. There are locks, however, that make breaking in such a nuisance that he'll go somewhere else. And such locks are not difficult to install in place of present hardware.

When you change a lock on a door, try to find one that matches the holes and mortises already there. If you can't, of if you want a bigger, tougher lock, fill the openings with cut-to-fit wooden plugs.

If you feel a replacement lock is necessary, visit a lock-smith or a *building* hardware dealer and get some professional help selecting the new hardware. (Most ordinary hardware stores don't handle the better-than-typical locks.) You'll find that the lock comes with a "templet" which you use to position all the holes and mortises.

In some cases, one or more of the holes or mortises required by the new lock may coincide with those of the old ones, particularly if they are by the same manufacturer. Holes and mortises that do not coincide must be filled with cut-to-fit plugs. It is worth the bother to cut the fillers so that the grain runs the same way as the surrounding wood, for greatest permanence. Fasten them in with glue, but without metal fasteners which might interfere with cutting the new holes and mortises. It may be necessary to fill the cutouts in the jamb, also, to accommodate the new strike.

Much more secure than typical house locks is one that has a deadlatch (pencil points to it here) that locks the latch in its extended position, so it cannot be slipped open by burglars. Look for this feature when you buy a new lock.

Even more secure is a dead-lock, shown protruding from door above the regular dead-latch. This bolt must be activated by a knob on the inside, and a key on the outside. Still better than this is a deadbolt which must be key-operated on either side.

With the fillers in place, follow the instructions that come with the lock. You may want to take care of any finishing problems to make the wood patches match before you finally install the new lock.

WHEN WEATHER STRIPPING DOESN'T STOP THE WEATHER

There is enough space around a properly hung access door to throw a snowball through, if you multiply an eighth of an inch or so by the distance around the door. This space is ordinarily filled with weather stripping of one form or another that through cushion-fit or spring-fit closes the gap. The most common types are foam plastic, plastic-sheathed jute or other soft cord, and metal. They can lose their springiness, all of them, and no longer do the job.

Fortunately, hardware and building supply stores now carry, almost universally, weather strip kits of sizes for both doors and windows, complete with instructions, all very easy to install either with adhesives or brads.

How do you tell when your weather stripping is no longer stopping the weather? By feel. On a day when the wind is blowing more or less right at the door, hold the palm of your hand along the edge of the door, across the top and the bottom. If you can feel coolness, your stripping isn't doing the job.

Some houses are equipped with weather stripping that can be adjusted, to snug it up against the door. Usually, you loosen some screws, push the material up, and tighten the screws. In other cases, you can accomplish the same thing by lifting brads, most often brass, and redriving them.

However, if the weather stripping itself is deteriorated, if the foam-plastic type or the plastic-sheathed jute type is compacted, it might be best to replace it. Modern varieties are made of better materials, including plastics that resist most stubbornly any tendency to go out of shape.

Many doors are installed without any weather stripping at the sill, which is a serious mistake. You can buy, at building supply outlets, a special type of stripping intended for the bottom edge of doors. There are several individual types, but most of them involve a mechanism which, when the door closes, pushes the sealing material down against the sill. Therefore, *it doesn't scrape on the sill and wear out*. Nor does it require any installation on the sill itself, which might cause someone to stumble and fall. Installation of such stripping is simple, as you'll notice when you read the instructions packaged with it.

STORM AND COMBINATION DOORS

If you have aluminum or other metal storm doors, you are being spared the trouble which often comes up with wooden doors. Because combination doors must be designed to allow interchange of screens and storm sash, because they are always fitted with closers often causing severe rack and twist strain, and because they must be of relatively light construction to stay within cost limitations, wooden doors tend to come loose at the joints after a few seasons.

The quick and easy way to handle this problem is to take the door down, clamp it tight together, and fasten strips of hardboard from edge to edge, holding it back just far enough to miss the doorstop on each side. If you put this reinforcement on the inside of the door, fastening it with small flathead screws and painting it to match the rest of the door, you'll never see it. But the door will be stronger than ever, with one strip across the top and a wider one across the bottom. Do the job in the spring or fall, halfway between the cold season and the insect season, and you can take your time at it.

2

WINDOWS AND SCREENS

EXCEPT FOR THE INSTANT problem of broken glass, most of the things that go wrong with windows and screens come along so gradually that you can anticipate trouble before it actually occurs. The best example is deteriorating putty. Although modern "glazing compounds" are relatively permanent and flexible, the putty of a few years ago tends to get brittle. With dimensional changes of the glass and the window sash, it gradually chips away. Eventually, it is all gone. If you spot this sort of deterioration in time, you can fix it at your leisure, before it becomes critical. The same is true of slowly deteriorating old window screens, now easy to improve with screening that lasts much, much longer.

TECHNIQUES OF GLAZING AND REGLAZING

Although installing new glass in a window has the look of daub-and-glob, there are some methods that make the job better and longer lasting.

• Have the glass cut about 1/8" or 3/16" smaller than the actual dimensions of the sash it goes into. This allows a little space on all sides for expansion and contraction. Naturally, the need for this space is greater with bigger sheets of glass, less for smaller sheets.

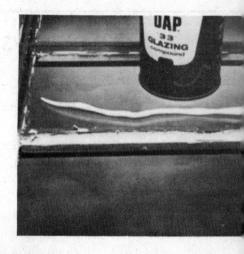

1. Apply glazing compound to the sash all around before you put the glass in place, so that it rests in a complete bed of compound. This is easiest to do if you roll compound into snakes between palms.

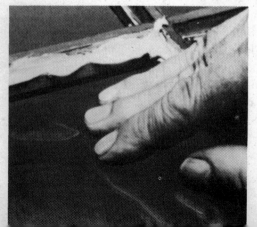

2. Position glass in the bed of compound; then gently press it into place. The material should ooze out beneath the glass and up around its edges. The excess below is easy to clean away.

• When you clean out the remains of the glass and putty being replaced (wear gloves handling the glass and be careful), be sure to clean it *all* out. In some cases, this may entail removing a few slivers of wood, but it is important. Otherwise, you will not be taking full advantage of the adhesion and flexibility of the glazing compound.

• Brush on a wood preservative such as "Woodlife" before you do anything else. This tends to stabilize the wood and forestall both rot and paint deterioration.

3. Glazier's points come in many different new shapes, including varieties you can push into the sash with the end of your glazing chisel. Apply them after glass is pressed into compound.

4. Regular triangular points may come packaged with a driving tool like this. If not, improvise with something like a 1/2" steel washer.

Seating the glass in the frame. It is a mistake merely to put the glass in place, drive glazier's points, and then putty. Properly done, you line the frame with glazing compound *first*. Then when you put the glass in, the compound will ooze up around the edges, so that the glass is *not in contact with the frame itself at any point*. When you finish the glazing, you'll have the glass "floating" in the glazing compound, sealing the opening completely against air and moisture, yet free to come and go with the elasticity of the compound.

As you handle glazing compound, you'll discover that it softens and becomes more plastic with manipulation and from the warmth of your hands. In a few seconds, a wad of the fairly stiff material scooped from the can is quite soft. You can roll it into a "snake" between the palms of your hands. And this is the key to compound application, both under the glass and in the troweled bevel on top. These are the steps:

1. Roll out snakes of compound and run them all around the opening, roughing them into place with thumb or finger. You don't need a lot of material in this operation, just enough to fill beneath the glass. Move as rapidly as is convenient, because the compound tends to reharden rather quickly once you stop manipulating it.

2. Position the glass in this bed of compound and carefully press down on it, so that it sinks into the material. If the glass is small, you can usually do this in a single operation, with your fingers spread to distribute the pressure. With larger glass work carefully along one side, then the next, and on around the pane. When this job is done properly, compound will ooze up around the glass, and it will also spread out beneath it, forming a little bead which you remove later.

3. Install the glazier's points. Although the time-honored

5. When the points are in, roll out more snakes of compound and glob them into place. Then use chisel or putty knife to smooth the bevel. As the photo shows, the knife should ridge the glass and the corner of the sash, at an angle of about 45 degrees. Excess compound peels off clean and easy.

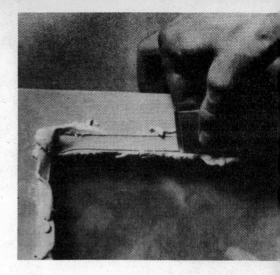

6. Paint over glazing compound should extend just barely on the glass, to seal it entirely. Easiest way to make this edge neat is with masking tape applied carefully to leave about $1/16''$ of glass exposed. Or, use special scraper with a shoulder that rides sill and leaves proper amount of paint on glass and a neat edge.

Old putty that has become brittle may not need to be removed entirely, but flaking sections should be cleaned to firm material with a glazier's chisel. Smooth glazing compound into the cavities and paint.

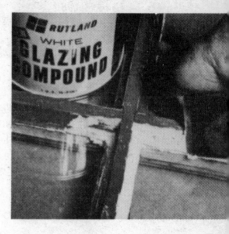

little metal triangles are still used, you'll find several different styles of points today, some of them easier to use. And you'll find some simplified methods of using them (see photos). Points spaced about 8″ apart will do the job on large panes, two to a side on smaller pieces of glass.

4. Soften up some more snakes of compound and press them into position. Then take your putty knife and, holding it as shown in the photograph, smooth out the bevel. Do not move the knife too fast; a slow trowelling movement pro-

duces the smoothest bevel. There should be a small ribbon of excess compound *on the glass* beyond the corner of the knife, as well as on the frame itself. This is assurance that the bevel is complete. The two little ribbons are easy to pull off without touching the bevel.

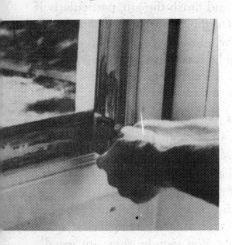 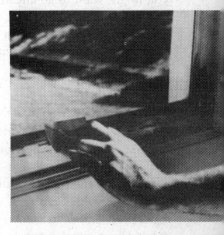

The most vulnerable areas of windows are the lower sills. Begin repair by scraping away loose paint down to bare wood, a two-handed job.

Sand rough spots with medium grit sandpaper, feathering edges of old paint to blend with bare wood surfaces. Follow up with fine sandpaper for a silk smooth surface.

Finish sill with good quality primer and interior paint. A properly painted window has 1/8" overlap of paint on the pane. Use of masking tape assures a straight edge.

5. Paint. Although some manufacturers of glazing compound approve the idea of painting immediately, it is no doubt better to wait a few days, to let the compound firm up and "skin over." The degree of convenience should be your guide in this decision. When it would be a nuisance to wait, you might want to go ahead and finish the job, particularly if you are using a latex paint. On the other hand, when you do a reglazing job on a storm window that doesn't have to go back on the house immediately, the wait would be worth the bother.

WHERE DO YOU WORK ON A WINDOW?

It's no fun, and it's not particularly safe, glazing a window at the top of a ladder. There are a half-dozen or so up-and-down trips, hanging on with one hand or with a knee hooked over a rung. And the tools you drop, not to mention the glass.

Of course, the problem disappears with storm sash. You take the window down, reglaze it, and put it back up. But what about regular windows? Fortunately, they are usually covered with screen or storm sash, thus protected and rarely broken. But when they do go, is it much of a job removing a window? Probably less of a job than you think. Many experts balance the removing window versus the ups-and-downs of doing repairs with the window in place this way:

If it's a ground floor window that you can reach from a stepladder, leave the window in. If it's a second story or higher window, calling for an extension ladder, take the window out.

How to remove a window. You can always remove a sash, either upper or lower, from inside. The way you do it de-

WINDOW CONSTRUCTION

Components of a window construction are illustrated in this drawing. The window sash slides up and down in channels formed by the stop and the parting strip, the parting strip and blind stop.

pends on how old the house is and how antiquated or up-to-date the windows are.

Starting with the oldest, there is a flat molding, called the "stop" that runs from the window sill to the top of the window frame, on either side. It forms the channel for the lower sash to ride in, teamed up with a square member called the "parting strip." On the far side of the parting strip is the channel for the upper sash, formed by the strip and an outside molding.

If you remove the stop on one side, you can lift out the lower sash. Then, if you remove the parting strip on the same side, you can lift out the upper sash.

Important: Virtually every window has sash weights (if

they're old enough) or spring-powered counterbalances. In the case of weights, you'll find that the sashcords are fastened into the side edges of the sash by means of a knot fitted into a slot. Lift out the cords and tie a loose overhand knot in each to keep it from being pulled into the window frame by the sashweight. The spring-type counterbalance is usually fastened to the bottom of the sash by means of some screws through an L. When you remove these screws, the L will start to rotate. That is because the adjustment tension of the spring is set by twisting the L when it is installed. Do not let the L spin free. Instead, let it unwind slowly and count the revolutions. That way, you'll be able to rewind the spring to the same tightness when you replace the window.

Since the stop has no doubt been painted over and is therefore stuck on, you probably have to work at it with a fairly broad chisel or a pinchbar. If you pry it loose from the back, that is, in the channel, any mars or scratches will be less visible than if you work from the front edge.

The parting strip is usually bedded in a groove in the window frame. Like the stop, it should be removed with the prybar applied to the outside, to minimize the damaged look.

In newer windows, the entire construction may be different. On both sides of the frame you'll find a metal or a plastic molding that forms the channels for the two windows and includes the counterbalancing mechanism. This device is only lightly fastened to the frame, often with a nail at the top and a staple at the bottom. If you remove the window stop and those fasteners on one side the entire thing slips out of the frame, freeing both upper and lower sash. All you have to do is take out the counterbalance screws, and the sash is free to go into the workshop where it's handy to work on the broken glass.

FAULTY WINDOW ACTION

Older windows, riding in wooden channels, are often hard to operate, because of the wood-against-wood friction. Even worse, sometimes, is wood-against-paint friction, and that is why it is standard painting advice never to paint in the channels. The worst kind of sticking comes when a paint job virtually glues the window in place. Conversely, a window is sometimes too loose.

Hard-riding windows can usually be loosened up with an application of stick lubricant, candlewax, or spray lubricant. Be sure to treat the edges of the window stop and the parting strip, as well as the bottom of the channel.

Paint-stuck windows. They'll usually break loose if you pound along the sides of the sash with the heel of your hand. It may be necessary, also, to use a screwdriver or small pry-bar at corners of the sash, prying against the frame to break the paint layer. Follow this with lubrication. In extreme cases, remove the window stop on both sides and jiggle the sash loose. (Metal or plastic window channels are, of course, never painted, nor do windows mounted in them very often stick.)

Air-leaking windows. These let in a lot of cold, and they should be weather stripped. As with doors, check the leakage when the wind is blowing against that side of the house, feeling along the edges and top and bottom and "meeting rail" for drafts. Building supply outlets sell special weather stripping for windows. The most common forms are metal, light and inconspicuous. When you install a strip on the back side of the lower sash meeting rail you never see it, yet it cuts down air leak between the two sashes. A strip on the bottom of the lower sash seals off the leak between it and the sill.

Rope-type weather stripping can be used around windows, and it is especially effective when the gap is large. Nailed to the lower *outside* edge of the lower sash, it will cork up any space between it and the sill. When air leaks at the edges of a window, you can seal it off by nailing strips snug against the outside of the sash frame.

Windows that rattle. Either because of shrinkage or wear, rattling windows are loose in their channels. You can tighten up the lower sash by removing the stop and renailing it closer to the sash. The proper spacing is about the thickness of a postcard, loose enough to slide, but not loose enough to rattle. It is more difficult to silence a noisy upper sash, because the parting strip can't be moved, and in some cases neither can the outside molding. The easy way to silence an upper sash is by cutting narrow strips of felt and cementing them to the back side of the parting strip.

WHEN A SASHCORD BREAKS

The counterbalancing systems of windows sometimes go bad, whether they are the modern spring-powered kind or the old-fashioned sash weight variety. Fixing the modern kind is simple. Fixing the old-fashioned kind is so difficult you may decide to convert to more up-to-date version.

When a window has a sashcord it works this way. The cord fastened to the edge of the sash, in a slot, rides up the inside of the frame, over a pully mounted in the frame, and disappears. Inside the frame the wood is fastened to an iron casting, a weight which helps you raise the window and helps hold it open at the top.

Over a period of time, the sashcord wears. And it may break. It or its function must be replaced. To do this, you must get into the frame, where the weight is.

If you'll examine the channels the sash rides in, you'll discover that near the bottom, there is an access method provided in one form or another. It may be a wooden insert. It may be metal. And it may be painted over so many times that it is all but invisible. When you remove it, you can reach in and pull out the sash weight. Next, remove the window (use instructions above) and you have both ends of the sashcord available, one tied to the weight, one inserted in the slot in the sash.

To replace the cord, whether it is broken or merely badly worn, cut a length of new cord the exact length of the old one. Slip one end over the pulley at the top of the window frame. By feeding it into the frame and jiggling it, you should be able to make the cord fall to the opening near the bottom. If necessary, tie a piece of string to the cord and feed it into the opening at the top, with a weight tied to the end. Fish out the weight at the bottom, then pull the string through, drawing the sashcord with it. Tie the end of the sashcord to the weight. Slip the cord into the slot in the sash. Put things back together.

There are variations to this. Many homeowners living in older houses are replacing sashcord with a special sash chain you can buy at building supply or hardware outlets. It lasts longer. Another variation is spring-powered counterbalances building supply dealers have, replacing the cord idea entirely. They are easier to install than sashcords are to replace and your dealer can give you specific tips for working with the kind he handles.

How to modernize the system. Since you must go to the bother of taking the window apart in order to replace sash-cords, and since it is shortsighted to fix one side of the window without doing the other, even though for some reason only one cord may need replacement, why not consider this idea.

At any good building supply outlet, you can buy the modern, metal or plastic glide-and-counterbalance units discussed above and solve a number of problems at one time. First, you end sticking problems; second, you end some weather stripping worries, and third, you get trouble-free counterbalancing.

The changeover is simple. You merely remove the stop and the parting strip. Cut the cord. If the pully in an old window interferes, remove it. Then, you slip the new system in place along with the sash, connect the counterbalance, and nail the stop back on.

Lock that mounts on the meeting rails is similar to old standby, but has a key that makes it tough on breakers-and-enterers. Even if they break glass, they may not have time — or want to risk time — to remove screws. Block that event with one-way screws you can buy at locksmith or hardware stores.

New version of meeting rail lock mounts at the corner of the window, with strikes on the upper sash. It can be engaged with window closed, with lower sash raised, with upper sash lowered, or both opened slightly. Thus, there is ventilation plus security.

For dormer windows, a lockable handle replaces the old one. In some cases this may require drilling out old rivets and installing new ones to mount handle.

MORE EFFICIENT WINDOW LOCKS

The standard window lock does very little to baffle a burglar who is very serious in his intent to break into your house. It's a simple matter of breaking out a small piece of glass, twisting the lock, and raising the window. Modern locks are available, however, that require a key and that are hard to jimmy since the keyhole is on the inside, where it can't be seen.

Generally, these locks are stocked by hardware stores. They install in the same way as the no-key kind, often using the same screw holes. They have a disadvantage, and it is one reason for the frequent ineffectiveness of such locks: You can't leave the window partly open for ventilation.

There is, however, a type of lock that differs from the standard, in that it goes at the side of the window. The main part, the bolt, of the lock screws on the top of the lower sash. The strike screws to the side of the upper sash, and *there are two strikes.* One of them goes a few inches above the other. Thus, you can open the window a few inches, but still lock it against further opening.

REPAIRING FAULTY SCREENS

Screens and screening are rarely subject to serious damage, and the problems they present call for a replacement more often than repair. The screening deteriorates. Moldings may rot away, even the frame may decay. All of these failings are likely to occur first at the bottom of a screen, where moisture lasts longest following rains, and where there may be accumulations of debris which encourage decay. For that reason, inspect screens, particularly at their bottom edges, once a year. Fortunately, you can usually take your time about repairs, when you find them. Screens are rarely a crisis problem.

Always paint the sash and cross members before you install screening, both to protect the wood and to prevent the possibility that bare wood may show through.

Replacing defective screens. Although there are many different kinds of window screen designs, those requiring replacement of the screening are usually pretty old and pretty much of simple construction. The frame is a square molding. The screen is held to the frame by means of tacks or more recently staples. The edge is covered with a delicate "screen molding."

In some cases there may be a groove under the screen molding. The screening is pressed into this groove by means of a "spline" which may be metal or wood. This system is excellent, because the spline not only holds the screen securely, but its action helps draw it tight.

The exact design of the screen will become apparent, of course, as you dismantle it to replace the screening. First, carefully lift off the molding. Use a small pinchbar or chisel. Apply the lift at the exact point where brads or staples occur, holding the molding down. Otherwise, it is almost sure to splinter. Then take out the tacks or staples holding the old screen. If it is a spline design, and the spline is metal, you may be able to lift it out intact and reusable. Wooden splines are almost sure to come out in pieces. If this is the case, and if you want to use the spline system on the new screen, you'll have to cut some splines to size from wood scrap.

New materials. Now being used for screening are fiberglass, aluminum, and plastic, which cost a trifle more, but whose permanence and ease of handling make them worth the small difference. When you buy the new screening, be sure the width and length are slightly bigger than the opening to be covered. This may make it necessary to buy screen one size wider (usually no more than 6″) than you actually need. But if

Staples are faster and handier than tacks in replacing screens.

you don't have the excess at the edge, you'll find it almost impossible to stretch the screen tight and smooth. There'll be nothing to hold on to.

There are no rules for putting new screen on a frame, but there are some procedures that make the job easier for most people. First, position the screen carefully at one corner, so that the molding will just cover it. Fasten it with one tack or staple at the corner and one an inch or so from the corner on both sides. This will anchor the screen firmly and let you stretch it tight.

Second, move to the adjacent corner on the longer side of the screen. Pull the material tight, really tight, and fasten it with the three-tack (or staple) system mentioned above. Then run fasteners along that edge, spacing them about 6" apart. Make sure that the wires of the screen run *exactly parallel to the side of the screen.*

Third, move to the other corner adjacent to the one you did first, pull the screening tight, and fasten it at the corner and every 6".

Principle of spline method of installing screening is shown in this mock-up. Spline is slightly smaller than the groove, and holds the screening slip-proof when it is pressed in place. The action of the spline tends to pull the screen tight.

You now have the screen fastened on two sides, and the excess you'll need for handling is on the other two sides. It may be, also, that there are a few large wrinkles, waves, in the screening, running diagonally. They will disappear when you pull the material tight in the other two directions.

Fourth, move to the free corner. Pull the screening diagonally toward that corner until the wrinkles disappear and you can see that the threads will come into parallel with the frame. You will probably have to line this up pretty much by eye at first, since a certain amount of "sag" toward the center is inevitable. Then, as you run fasteners along the remaining two sides, you can apply the amount of tension required to bring the screening and the frame into parallel.

Fifth, nail the screen molding back in place. If it was badly damaged when you lifted it, buy new molding. *Paint it before you install it,* to save a lot of tedious cutting along the screen. When you're replacing a molding, if you use brads one size larger than the originals but no longer, they'll hold tight.

All that remains now is to cut off the excess screen, running a sharp blade along the edge of the screen molding.

Replacement with a spline. If the screening was originally held in place with a spline, you have two choices. You can replace it with a spline, or you can forget the spline and do the job with tacks or staples as outlined above. This may be the better choice if wooden splines were ruined when you took them out. If you decide to go with the splines, the procedure is a little different from that involving fasteners, since you can't use the same tightening techniques. Follow these steps:

First, position the screening at one corner so that it overlaps the grooves on both members of the frame by a distance about equal to the width of the grooves. Force the spline in on the shorter of these two sides. Start at one end and pull the material as tight as possible as you work the spline in progressively toward the opposite corner.

Second, move to the opposite side, where you have an

It may not always be necessary to replace an entire screen. If the half on either side of the crossbar is okay, lift the molding, cut across the bar, and remove only the bad screening.

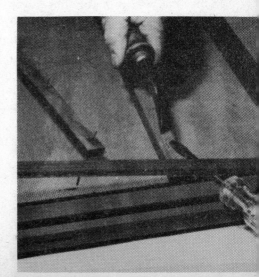

overlap of screen to pull on. Make it tight beneath spline, then force the spline into the groove. You'll find that the action of the spline draws the screen up to its final tightness.

Third, force the spline into one of the remaining two sides, lining it up carefully with the frame.

When there's a cross member. Use a sharp knife to cut the screen across the cross member, leaving the fasteners holding that part of the material you'll leave in place. Lift the fasteners from the screen to be removed. These may be splines or tacks or staples, but there is normally never a spline across the cross member.

Lap the new screening over the old at the cross member, and do the rest of the job as covered above.

Repairing a hole. When a screen has a hole in it, but is otherwise in good condition, you can patch it with a small piece of screening as shown in the accompanying photographs.

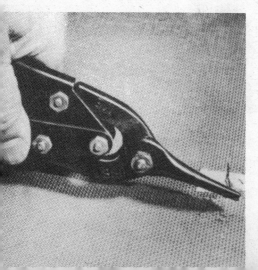

1. Cut the hole into a true rectangle, cleaning up the ragged edges. Tin snips or even a pair of household shears will do this job.

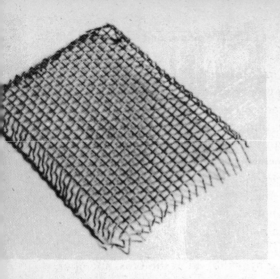

2. Cut a patch of screening material a little bigger than the hole, then strip away two or three strands on all four edges. Bend the resulting strand ends 90 degrees downward. An easy way to do this is over the edge of a table.

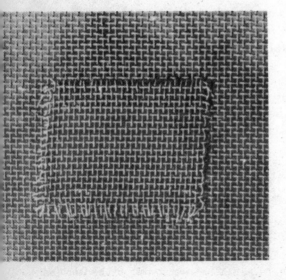

3. Lay the patch over the hole, and maneuver the strands through the screen. Then, bend the ends of the screen fibers, to hold the patch in place. It will be barely visible.

3

ROOF REPAIRS

DAMAGE TO A ROOF — even if it is small in itself — is often directly responsible for tremendous damage inside the house. It doesn't take much of a leak overhead to make ceiling plaster fall, floorboards warp, wallpaper peel off, and more, during a three-day rain.

Since a rainy day is about the worst kind of an environment for roof repairs, there is a well-founded adage in the world of home repair; the right time to fix a leak in the roof is *before it starts to leak.*

This is an even greater truth in view of the fact that a small leak may exist for years without revealing itself in the form of dripping water. Meanwhile, it is letting moisture into the inner structure of the house, causing mildew and decay where you can't see it until, one day, something caves in.

As with any other phase of preventive maintenance, anticipating roof troubles before they start must depend on careful periodic inspection. And, of course, you must know what to be on the lookout for.

All roofing materials deteriorate, although some of them go faster than others. Rain, hail, sleet, snow, heat of sun, freezing weather, wind—all these have their effect. Add the damage done by tree branches that overhang the roof.

HOW TO WATCH FOR DETERIORATION

You can do a fairly worthwhile inspection job, of a fairly new roof, from the ground. Use field glasses if you have them handy. But you must go up on the roof if there are indications of trouble.

Wooden shingles. Cedar shingles follow a set pattern of color change from the day they are laid. To begin with, they are a light reddish brown. This color fades, at first, until the shingles are a silvery gray. This is caused not only by bleaching of the natural pigments in the cedar, but also by the way some of the colorants dissolve in rain water and leach out.

From the day the shingles have turned their lightest (usually the first year) they start to darken, taking on an increasingly deeper gray color. Eventually, they become a gray so dark it turns quite black when the shingles are wet.

The thing to watch for, in your inspection from the ground, is differences in color change, variations from the norm. If a patch of shingles shows a color unlike the surrounding area, the reason is usually an accumulation of moisture under the shingles. You can check on this by watching the roof dry, as

DEFECTS TO LOOK FOR IN WOODEN SHINGLES

Among the most serious defects is a split in a shingle directly over the joint between two in the next row.

Shingles as badly warped, cupped, eroded, split, and mildewed as these (and of a low grade, in the first place) may have to be replaced, although spraying with wood preservatives may give them added years of leak-free life.

Erosion shows up best at the base of a row. Shingles shown here have lost about $3/16''$ of thickness.

These shingles, brittled by age and showing other typical signs of deterioration, have been walked on—and the broken shingle shows the type of damage that results from trafficking over an old roof. That explains the use of cherry pickers to work from.

Less common is insect damage, always out of sight back in the overlap of the shingles. Sometimes you can detect it when sawdust-like bits of wood wash out from beneath the rows.

Composition shingles show their age and deterioration mainly through alligator-like crazing. This means the shingles are brittle; a strong wind could break the flaps loose, unless they are cemented down securely. Roof spraying specialists can rejuvenate shingles like this.

it dries after a rain. If there is an area that stays darker in color—that is, wet-looking longer—it is fairly certain that there is water under the shingles. This water may be causing no damage; it may never cause any damage. But the area becomes suspect and should be checked periodically.

As a wood shingle roof starts to age, there are other things to watch for:

• Cupped or dished shingles usually take their form from water beneath. They dry faster on the outside, and the wood shrinks. Cupping also may be caused by the use of inferior-grade shingles, a few of which may slip into the job even when top materials are specified.

• Splits in shingles may be caused by too much space between them, by improper nailing, by widths that are too great. Aging and weathering contribute.

• Worn and weathered shingles are merely showing the ravages of time. However, the wear may be greater in some shingles than others. Most often the shingles' that are cut "flat to the grain" erode faster than those which expose the edge grain of the cedar. It is easy to check the actual amount of weathering a shingle has undergone by examining it *close to the butt of the shingle just above it*. There will be little or no reaction to the weather at the exact point where the shingle emerges from the one above it. But, there will be a sharp "dip" to the new, worn level—a good indication of the amount of wood that has weathered away.

Composition shingles. A composition shingle is formed of a "felt" of asphalt-and-fiber, on the surface of which there are granules of a mineral material. These granules give the shingles their fire resistance—and their color.

Deterioration comes slowly, in several ways. The base gradually decomposes, eroding away under the elements, with the passage of time. The granules may, as a part of this decomposition, gradually loosen and wash away. A certain amount of brittleness may develop with time, causing the shingles to break away in small pieces. And, if the wind is violent, the flaps may raise and tear loose. Finally, there may be a change in color—partly because of fading of the coloration in the minerals, partly because the minerals wash away.

Composition shingles tend to deteriorate in a rather uniform degree, owing to the homogeneous nature of their construction. All the shingles on a given exposure usually need replacing if any of them do. And, one exposure (south or west) may need replacement before areas subjected to less abuse from the weather (north or east).

However, there are examples of physical damage that may make replacement of a single shingle unit necessary.

IF YOU GO UP ON THE ROOF

Two things to remember when you go up on the roof for repairs or for examination:

• You can damage the roof rather seriously tramping around on it after the shingles have aged enough to be brittle. Therefore, keep your traffic to a minimum.

• You can damage yourself—especially if it's a two-story house. Older roofs grow more and more slippery, especially composition shingles with granules that are coming loose.

Be careful. Wear rubber soles. A roof is dangerous *if you find it unnerving to walk up or down it without using your hands to make a quadruped of yourself.* It is not how steep the roof actually is; it's how steep it seems to you.

If you find the roof uncomfortable, use the trick (see photo) of hanging a ladder over the peak, working up and down it on both sides, then moving it along to the next position where work is necessary.

Even when the roof is not particularly steep, and you don't mind working on it, try to keep the ladder you came up directly below where you are working. If you should lose your balance, you'll have a chance to grab it before you go over the edge.

One more thing: Do not climb over the end of a ladder onto the roof. Make sure there is enough ladder extending above the eaves so that you can climb the ladder high enough to step off the side. The danger involved here is not so much the chance that you'll fall climbing off the ladder to the roof. Instead, you're likely to fall trying to get back on the ladder if it doesn't extend far enough past the eaves so that you can mount it safely from the side.

This ladder trick makes roof work safer. Clamp two stubs of 2 x 4 to the rail, just below a rung, angled to hang over the ridge.

THE BASIC REPAIR DECISION

There are three stages of roof deterioration, when your objective is to prevent serious damage to your home.

1. You may be able to replace a few shingles and put things back in shape again.

2. You may be able to contract for a rejuvenation job.

3. You may have to call in a roofing contractor and have the whole thing done anew.

When wear is extensive, what you hope for is the second procedure. Both wood shingles and those made of asphalt composition can be given new life—enough to make the investment truly worth while. The technique most often used is to spray a wood preservative on cedar shingles, a solvent on composition roofing which softens asphalt, giving it new life. The men who do the job work from cherry pickers, and properly never put a foot on your roof. You can find a roof renovator in the yellow pages.

Since the men who do renovating are interested in a successful job (most of them guarantee their work), they will not ordinarily work on a roof that is too far gone to be revived by their services. For that reason, it is almost the best idea to call on one for an estimate and an appraisal. His decision may determine for you the need for a new roof.

So effective are life-extending treatments for roofs that you should consider a treatment for a new roof, if you have the job done over completely or if you are living in a fairly new house. The use of Cuprinol or Pentox or other preservatives based on pentachlorphenol can double the life of wood shingles, and sometimes more than double their life.

If you want to increase the life of composition shingles,

many authorities recommend two coats of a high-grade acrylic house paint sprayed on the roof. Such paints as Moore-Guard, Lucite, K-100 and other acrylic formulas will dry over asphalt (an oil paint won't) and add protection for the house itself. Don't overlook the opportunity to pick your color, if you have this job done—or do it yourself. Most home experts these days vote for white or quite light colors on the roof, as a means of cutting down on the amount of heat your attic picks up on a sunny day. On the other hand, you may decide on a color that enhances the looks of your house—or the whole neighborhood.

HOW TO REPLACE WOOD SHINGLES

Since every row of shingles must overlap the one next below it, they must be laid from the bottom up. The men who built the house and roofed it started with a double row at the eave line. Then they laid the next row, and the next, and the next, until they reach the ridge. (In actual practice, this may be done in the form of a pyramid or triangle, in order to increase efficiency and to allow two men to work as a team.)

Principles of proper shingling are shown in this layout. No crack lies above another crack. Each shingle overlaps the one below it by slightly more than half its length, so that there is actually double overlap at the thin upper end of the shingles. This is why you must buy replacement shingles of the same length as those already in place.

The nails in each row are driven high enough in the shingle so that the next row above overlaps it. This prevents water from leaking through the nails because each nail is overhung by the shingle above it. While this is as sound a method of construction as you can think of from the standpoint of weatherproofness, it makes replacing shingles a little difficult. The accompanying photographs help to illustrate the procedures. (They were shot on a "staged" roof, owing to the difficulties of making photographs on an actual roof.)

First, dig out the damaged shingle, using a chisel to split it into narrow strips. If it was nailed properly, there are two nails up there under the next shingle, usually a little less than one quarter of the shingle's width in from each edge. Therefore, all the narrow strips will pull out easily except those which may happen to have the nails through them. Keep at it until everything splits free.

Pick out a shingle that is the proper width, or rip a wider one to size. It should fit easily between the two adjacent shingles, ideally with about ⅛" of space on each side.

Shove the shingle up into the space where it is to go, until the thin end hits the nails. Give it a couple of taps so those nails make two marks at the end. Pull the shingle out, and use a saw to *cut two slots parallel to the edges* at the point where the nails made their marks. The length of these slots should be just enough to let the shingle slide past the nails into position, but no longer. One way to make sure the slots are the right length is to check them against one of the scraps of the old shingle that has its nail mark in it. Another way is to slip the shingle into position when the slots are about right and continue cutting until they are.

There is an alternative method of handling the problem

of those nails. With a metal-cutting blade in a keyhole saw, or with one of those little hacksaw blade holders (see photo) you can work up under the butt of the shingle and cut the nails off. You must hold the saw so that it cuts fairly close to the surface, or the nails will still give you trouble.

In order to fasten the new shingle in place, you must break one of the basic rules of roofing and drive a nail that is exposed to the weather. It should be one nail, in the middle of the shingle, just a little above the butt. To keep this nail from becoming a leaking spot, put a dab of roofing cement or other calking material over its head.

Another method of securing the shingle in place is with a mastic-type adhesive. Spread a thick "sausage" of mastic on the bottom of the shingle. Keep the butt elevated as you push it in, then press the shingle down to bring the mastic into contact.

Repairing a larger area. If you discover damage to an area covered by many shingles, you use the above splitting technique only for those along the top row of the damage. The rest of the shingles can be ripped off any old way. An excellent tool for the job is a square-nose shovel or spade. Shove it under the butts and pry up. When the shingles are all off, use a hammer or wrecking bar to pull the nails.

In this operation, be careful not to damage the roofing felt. If you do dig through this—or if it is in bad shape anyway—replace it, slipping the new stuff under the edge of the sound felt at the top and edges, letting it lap over the felt at the lower side of the repair job.

When you buy the shingles for this repair work, one thing is important: *they must be the same length* as those used on

1. Split shingle in the middle of this picture puts a crack right over the joint in the row below. It should be replaced.

2. Use a chisel and hammer to split the shingle into strips you can pull out.

3. Shove a new shingle up into place until its end strikes the nails that held the shingle you removed. Then saw a kerf parallel to the shingle edges where each of the nails made its mark. This lets you shove the new shingle into place, the slots riding up the nails.

4. An alternate method of getting past those nails is by hacksawing them off close to the surface. This, however, is not as simple as the method covered above.

5. When the new shingle is in place, drive one nail through it in the center, 1″ or 2″ up from the butt.

6. Make that nail weatherproof by putting a dab of roofing calk, or other weatherproof calk-patch material.

the house originally. Otherwise, gaps will develop as you lay successive rows. Sometimes a building supply dealer will have a "broken" bundle" of shingles and will sell you a handful. On other cases, you may have to buy an entire bundle, which might be the best idea, all in all. You can store them away for the next time you need to work on the roof.

Now you're in the shingling business. To keep the new shingles lined up, obtain a straight length of 1 x 4 or so, long enough to reach completely across the repair area. Position it against the butts of the shingles on the sides of the patch. Use a chalk or pencil to mark a line across. The butts of the new shingles go along this line.

Start at the bottom. *Making sure that you do not put one joint over another,* fit a row of new shingles across the lower edge of the patch. Use two nails to a shingle, each one in from the edge a little less than one quarter of the shingle's width. These nails go in a row crosswise, that will be covered by an inch or two of the next course of shingles. You'll discover that each nail goes through the shingle it is holding in place, and also through the thin end of the shingle below it. Thus, each nail goes through two shingles, binding them together, sound and weathertight.

Continue to use the straightedge, so that the butts line up properly. At the top of the patch, split out the shingles and fit in the new ones as described above.

WORKING ON COMPOSITION SHINGLES

Composition shingles are just about completely homogenous, as compared to wooden shingles which vary considerably from one to another. That is why a composition roof is likely to deteriorate uniformly from gable to gable and ridge to eave, except for physical damage caused by wind or abrasion. Like wooden shingles, however, composition roofs suffer the most deterioration fastest on southern and western exposures, compared to eastern and northern. Keep this in mind when you inspect the roof.

These roofs are further "unitized" by the form of the shingles, which are usually in strips, rather than single. In addition, they may be designed to interlock in ways that make them more weathertight.

Because of these factors, it is rarely necessary to replace more than an occasional flap, torn loose by the wind or other stresses. In these cases, you do not remove anything, and you can often make use of the loose flap, if you can find it.

To begin with, if a flap is raised, but not detached, use roofing cement to fasten it back down. There may be a little separation at the crease; in that case, smear some cement along the crack.

Even if a flap is completely detached, you can replace it by cementing it in place and filling the crack.

Damage caused by strong winds raising the flaps of composition roofs is just about eliminated with special dabs of adhesive. After installation, the overlapping shingle bonds to the adhesive patches. If you have flap-raising troubles with your roof, you can buy a special cement that seals them down, applied with an ordinary calking gun (*right*).

Easiest method of replacing a missing flap in composition roofing is to slip a piece of aluminum or copper or galvanized steel into the roof, in place of the flap. See text for methods of replacing an entire composition strip.

When a flap is lost completely, the best method of repair is to cut a piece of sheet metal (copper, aluminum, or galvanized) more or less this size: twice the height of the flap plus 2″, by the width of the flap plus 4″.

Slip this piece of metal into the space left by the missing flap, with its edges under the adjacent shingles and shove it up until its upper edge is under the next shingle above.

Cement the metal in place, and cement the adjoining shingles to it. If the spot is conspicuous, paint it a camouflaging color, using a coat of primer followed by housepaint or exterior semigloss enamel.

Repairing larger areas. Should you find it necessary to replace an entire composition shingle unit, or more, try to save the job until a hot day, so that the shingles are at their most flexible. You can, except in quite cold weather, soften a shingle area with a heat lamp or photoflood in reflectors.

You will usually be able to raise the heat-softened shingles above the damaged strip far enough to get at the row of nails. Use a pinch bar to pull them. The strip may still be held by nails farther up under the shingles above, but those nails are so close to the edge that you can pull the strip loose.

Now, use the old strip *as a pattern to cut out notches* on the new piece where those nails near the edges were located. This will let you slip the new strip up into position. With the flaps still raised, you can drive new nails. Come close to the old nail holes, but try to miss them so that the new nails get a good grip on the new wood. Finish up by cementing down the flaps.

WHAT TO DO WHEN A ROOF REALLY LEAKS

When you discover that a roof leaks, it is most often because you discover the evidence of it in some living area of the house, in the attic, or in some under-eave area. It would be normal to expect the leak to be directly above the evidence. This is just about never the case, since the water had to run down a few rafters and along the underside of some roof sheathing and so forth, before it came to light. For this reason, the location of a leak *in the roof* bears little relationship to the location of the leak below. Instead, all you know for sure is that the leak is *uphill* from the place where it shows up.

The first move toward finding the leak is to make a careful search—while it is leaking—for the path the water takes. Examine sheathing, framing, and other construction members uphill from the place where the leak shows up. Trace it, if possible, to its origin.

If you can't do this, here is a trick:

1. Establish a point on the roof directly over the leak inside.

2. Pull a garden hose up on the roof and start soaking it down beginning at the point you estimate to be over the trouble area inside. If there is any doubt about being directly

over it, start soaking the roof at a point several feet below as a safety measure. Conduct this soaking over a width of perhaps 10'.

3. Gradually — very gradually — raise the soaking operation. A row of shingles at a time is a good gauge.

4. Post an associate inside, ready to note the very first sign of water coming through to the inside surface, with instructions to let you know the moment it does.

5. When he gives the signal, make a note of the point to which your roof-soaking has progressed. It will be very close to the point where rain water is entering your house.

It is important to move upward with your soaking very, very *slowly*. Otherwise, the first sign of a leak may actually come from water that you sprayed on the roof a distance below, but which took a little while to make its way through.

With the general area of the leak now established, begin examination of the roofing material, in search of the cause. Replace shingles and roofing paper as covered above in the discussions of wood or composition, as the case may be.

As the relative complexity of the foregoing may indicate, the job of locating and repairing an active roof leak is not one of the simplest home repair jobs. If your home is fairly new, the man who built it may feel it within his range of responsibilities to give you a hand with a leak that quite likely may be his fault. If your home is older, you may decide that it would be wiser and easier and safer to call in a roofing specialist.

RIDGES, VALLEYS, AND FLASHING

Thus far in roofing repair techniques, the problem has been with a single roof plane. There also are ridges, valleys, and

The metalwork above a chimney that emerges from a pitched roof is called a "cricket." Be sure to examine it when you check the roof for damage. As shown here, the pieces of roofing are missing which should cover the exposed triangle. Also, check where the cricket is mortared into the chimney bricks and tuckpoint new mortar in if necessary.

flashing. They represent only a small part of roofing area, but they can bring up special problems since their job is always to bridge the gap between two non-continuous surfaces. Here are the ways:

• The ridge is the peak of the roof, always there unless the house happens to have a single-pitch roof.

• Valleys occur between two downward-sloping roof areas. A gable, for example, produces a valley on either side.

• You find flashing where a roof meets other construction areas. A wing on a house, a single-story element against a two-story house, a shed roof off a wall of the house—these and similar construction elements usually produce a situation where the roof meets siding or other exterior wall material. Flashing is also the means of joining the roof to a chimney.

These elements of a roof do not present problems very often. The unusual problems involved in their construction invite special attention from the craftsmen who build the house. Because it is harder to do the job, the job is usually done better.

The standard method of handling ridges in original construction is with the same material that is used for the entire roof. That is to say, in a composition roof the ridge between

Damage to the ridge of a roof is most likely due to branches or trees. Cut them back, patch with trowel-on cement.

one plane and another will be formed of composition material. Most often, a wood-shingle roof will have wood as the spanning medium from one plane to another.

Valleys and flashings are different. In these situations the cross-over material is most often metal—aluminum, copper, or galvanized steel. The metal is bent to form a sort of trough down which water runs. Since the trough extends up beneath the shingles (or siding, in the case of flashing) there is little chance of a leak. The shingles or siding shed the water into the trough, where it sluices rapidly down to the eaves. When there is trouble, it is usually due to deterioration of the metal trough or blockage due to debris.

Repairing ridges. The ridge of a roof has things easy. All the water it must handle is the immediate rainfall on it. No water drains to it. It is at the top. Therefore, the ridge rarely needs work unless there is damage from branches of trees or other physical damage. On a wood-shingle roof, the ridge is most often a pair of boards, usually nailed over the tops of the final row of shingles. If, because of damage or weathering, these boards need to be replaced, it is a simple matter to rip them off and replace them with new stock. You'll probably eliminate the need for ever doing the job again if you flood the boards with wood preservative on sides, edges, and ends before you put them in place — with aluminum or galvanized nails.

The ridge of a composition roof is composed of a row of composition shingles, laid astraddle the ridge, overlapping each other with the nails of each shingle covered by the next.

When any of the segments are damaged, it is easy to raise the corners of the next shingle, lift the nails, and remove the defective material. As with run-of-the-roof shingles, it is easiest to do this on a hot day, or with the warmth of a heat lamp to soften the composition.

REPAIRING FLASHING MATERIALS

It is not often necessary to replace flashing completely. Most of the time, the damage is due to rust or erosion of the metal. Occasionally you may find joints separated, probably because of the stresses caused by ice freezing.

Rusted flashing. When a flashing material is galvanized steel, found especially on older buildings, there is certain to be some rust. Check your flashings to see, and if you discover any brown coloration that would indicate rust, buy a can of good quality metal *primer and topcoat in latex*. This should dry fast enough so you can get the job done quickly.

There may be spots where the metal has rusted through, or nearly through. Cut patches of the same kind of metal large enough to cover such spots with an overlap of 2″ or 3″. Carefully bend the patches to conform with the curve of the flashing. Use heavy paste-form roof patching cement to fasten the patches in place. If, in your judgment, the rest of the flashing metal indicates a considerable amount of deterioration, use a brush-on roofing cement to coat it completely, including the new patches.

Aluminum and copper flashing. Flashing made of these metals is not subject to rust in the same way as galvanized steel, and for that reason does not need repair so often. However, the life of both can be prolonged by a coating of paint. Check with your paint dealer for a primer specifically recommended for these metals; some primers are not intended for use on copper or aluminum.

Important: If you patch holes in copper or aluminum, be sure to use copper or aluminum. Do not use steel or iron. If you do, you'll set up a situation in which electrolysis will cause rapid decomposition of the metal.

Repairing joints. Copper flashing usually has soldered joints; galvanized steel sometimes does. However, crimping is common on galvanized steel, and it is always used on aluminum. Either way, when a joint separates, the two elements may pull apart far enough so that an overlap patch is necessary.

The easiest roof repair job is done with a calking gun and a tube-form material that has enough body to form a good bead. You may want to use a putty knife to trowel the material smooth after you've gunned it into place.

When the joint is widely separated, cut a patch of the same metal and cement it in place, as discussed above under Rusted Flashing.

WHERE FLASHING JOINS NON-ROOF AREAS

The standard method of installing flashing at points where roofing meets another material involves the "overlap" principle of shingling itself. The metal, bent to fit in place, extends well beneath the shingles. It is installed first, then shingles are laid over it.

On the non-roof surface, the flashing extends well beneath the siding or other material. Again, the metal is positioned, then the siding is nailed over it. Any repair work involves only replacing the siding material, making sure the flashing is secure beneath it.

When the non-roof material is brick, the problem is tougher. The flashing extends under the shingles, but it is bent and mortared into the bricks, whether they be structural or chimney bricks. Because of temperature changes from hot sun to freezing, the mortar often loosens between the bricks where the flashing goes. Although this can be repaired by chipping out the loose mortar and troweling in new, it is better to use a flexible calking material. Its flexibility stands a chance of longer survival than the brittleness of mortar. Be sure to chip away all loose mortar before calking.

The plumbing vent. One more area where a roof may give you trouble is around the plumbing vent—that stubby length of 3″ or bigger pipe that sticks up through the roof a few inches. Its purpose is to prevent air-locks and blockage in the plumbing system. The most common type includes a collar and flange that fits around the pipe, under the shingles above, and over those below.

Now and then, owing to expansion and contraction of the

The stack (air vent) of your plumbing system may spring a leak, which is easy to repair with brush-or-trowel roofing patch.

plumbing "stack," the collar may come loose from the pipe. If it does, trowel-on roofing cement makes a simple repair.

HOW TO KEEP
RAIN-CARRYING EQUIPMENT
AT WORK

LIKE YOUR ROOF, your gutters and downspouts are out of sight, and for that reason so often out of mind that they go neglected. Minor, easy-to-fix damage or deterioration grows until simple repair becomes complicated.

That is why rain-carrier maintenance and repair always begin with an inspection twice a year.

WHAT TO INSPECT

Every fall after the leaves have fallen and every spring when it warms up, make an inspection of the system from a ladder.

You are looking for these things:

• Collected debris that not only interferes with free movement of the water but can also contribute to corrosion. There should be relatively little debris if you have taken the wise precaution of installing *leaf guards over the gutters.* These guards are screens in one form or another that you slip under the lowest row of shingles. The screen covers the top of the eaves trough. Any leaves or other debris of a sizeable nature sluices over the screen, while the water passes through and down the system. Leaf guards are more effective than simple sieves at the top of each downspout, because they keep the entire system, not merely the downspouts, clean.

• Rusted areas in the inside of the gutters, which should always be repaired as soon as possible, before the extent of the damage is so great that a whole section may have to be replaced.

• Evidence that pools of water have dried in the gutters, instead of running on down the system. Take a whiskbroom along the gutters if they are quite dirty, and look for the long oval-shaped area of encrusted sediment that indicates repeated pooling and drying.

IMPROPER DESIGN
CAUSES QUICK DETERIORATION

Peeling paint is often a sign of more serious troubles. In this corner, with two roof areas above it, there should be a downspout. Overflowing water has contributed to paint failure in this area.

The streaks down over this gutter are a result of runover, caused by a low spot in the middle of a run which is too long in the first place.

One downspout (off the picture to the left) has the job of handling all the runoff from the dormer at the right plus all the roof—and it's too much. There should be a downspout where the stubend empties into the gutter.

• Mechanical failures show up in several ways. Joints may be forced apart by frost. Hangers may be loosened by the weight of snow and ice or water during a downpour. Downspouts may have separated from their connections at the ends of runs. This doesn't happen often when the joints are riveted, and therein lies the answer to repair. Force the joints back together, and use sheet metal screws or rivets to make them strong enough so it won't happen again.

• Paint failure on the outside of the gutters and downspouts is, of course, visible from the ground. However, there may be deterioration of coatings on the insides, too. You can't find it if it's inside downspouts where you can't see, and where it is quite rare, anyway. But you'll save work and money if you can catch finish failure on the inside surfaces of gutters. It is standard and sensible practice to brush-coat the gutters with roofing cement every year or so. This is simpler than taking care of the corrosion you may encounter if gutter linings go bad.

• A less common but serious type of rain-carrier damage is the downspout split by entrapped water that freezes and expands. When this happens, downspouts are finished and must be replaced.

The specific repair and maintenance techniques for each of these problems are covered below. It will be easier for you to handle them, however, if you first run down the mechanics and engineering of rain-carrier systems.

KINDS OF RAIN-CARRYING EQUIPMENT

Gutters are made in two basic shapes: half-round, and "K" style, the kind with the square back and the ogee front.

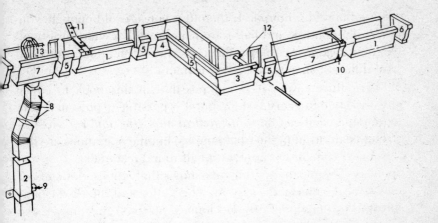

Modern rain-carrying equipment is composed of slip-together components, both in the K style shown here and in half-round. You can buy any of the elements individually for repair, and replacement, or for a new installation.

1. Gutter.	7. Outlet section.
2. Downspout.	8. Elbow.
3. Outside corner.	9. Pipe band.
4. Inside corner.	10. Clip-around hanger.
5. Slip-joint connector.	11. Strap hanger.
6. End cap.	12. Spike and ferrule hanger.
	13. Squirrel cage.

Downspouts are round and rectangular with rounded corners, sometimes plain and sometimes with corrugations. The elements are aluminum, galvanized steel, plastic, copper, or wood (except downspouts), as well as some less common materials not often used residentially. Although the K style is growing more and more popular, you still find a lot of half-round on older houses. If the older house is old enough, you may find both K and half-round, along with a wide variety of hangers, joints, corners, and caps, not to mention a number of different shapes in the downspouts.

For this reason, it is not possible in this book to cover every style in every system, but it is possible to present repair guidance that can be *translated to any situation*. K style elements are used in the photographs, but the operations are the same if you are working with half-round materials.

The accompanying drawing shows the various elements of a typical rain-carrier system. The gutter and the downspout come in lengths of 10' and longer, up to 30' in some cases. All of the elements slip together with special fasteners as shown in the photographs (there are similar slip connectors for half-round).

If you decide that the best method of repair is replacement of a length of gutter or downspout — or part of a length — or of one of the connectors, corners, or outlet sections or caps, you may want to take the damaged element to your building supply dealer and have him give you what you need to replace it. What he gives you may not be identical in appearance, but it will be identical in performance.

Important: Do not mix other metals with galvanized iron elements. If you do, you may run into excessive corrosion due to electrolysis, that is, galvanic action that takes place when iron or steel is in contact with another metal. This applies to rivets, fasteners, and other elements. Use steel with steel, aluminum with aluminum. If circumstances suggest or dictate the use of plastic with steel no electrolysis will result, as long as the fasteners, etc. are steel.

It has been the experience of many homeowners that

Slip-together elements make rain-carrying systems easy to assemble. Virtually any repair can be done by replacing a part, in K style as shown here or in half-round.

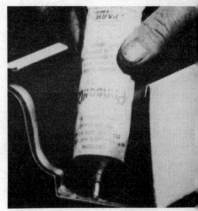

Units are a snug fit, calling for a rubber mallet to force them together. Gutter cement must be used to insure a watertight joint. Be sure the rivets or screws you use are of the same metal as the gutter and connector.

wooden gutters are inefficient because of the relatively small channel compared to the exterior size. When wood gutters begin to check, split, peel, and rot, it's time to think of replacing them with one of the other materials. Putting up a whole new gutter is no more than a one-man job, since the elements are so light in weight (particularly aluminum) that one man can handle them, even up at eave height.

Wooden gutters are difficult to repair. The photo above shows how an end cap of wood can be nailed over a rotted gutter end. Wood rot like that at the joint of two gutter pieces (*below*) is so difficult that replacement with a metal gutter is easier.

BASIC RAIN-CARRIER ENGINEERING

Rain-carrying systems are based on the convenient fact that water runs downhill. As long as there is a continuous downward pitch, the system will deliver the water. However, the more water the greater the pitch must be, or the greater the size of the eave troughs must be, or both. To stay within workable limits, these guidelines have been set up for rain-carrier installations.

• You need a downspout for every 500 square feet of roof area.

• You need a downspout for every 20' of gutter. In other words, if a run is much longer than 20', it should be high in the middle, with a downspout at each end.

• You need ½" of pitch, that is, downward slope, for every 20' of gutter run. A full inch is better. There are reasons for this. First, the pitch should always be steep enough to carry water to the downspout rapidly. Otherwise, it may fill the trough and run over.

Second, the movement of the water should be strong enough to carry along normal dust and dirt in the gutter. Third, the pitch should be enough to eliminate puddles and pools of water between rains, since lingering wetness means more corrosion and rust.

• Downspouts should have as few bends, elbows, as possible, since the curves increase the chance that leaves and other solids washing down the system will clog things, blocking the movement of the water.

• At the foot of every downspout you need some means of delivering the water away from the foundation. This may be splash blocks, deliberate grading, or underground piping. If you don't have it, the buildup of water is likely to produce basement leaks and deterioration of foundations.

It is reasonable to expect, although not at all a certainty, that the builder of your home followed the engineering principles when he put up the rain-carrying equipment. However, if performance fails repeatedly, it may be necessary for you to modify the system.

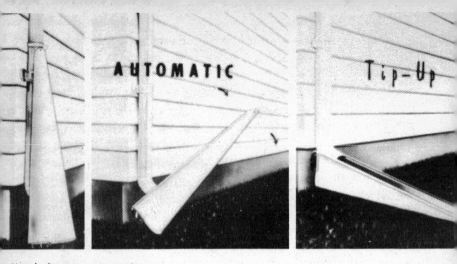

AUTOMATIC   Tip-Up

Metal downspout extensions
stay up when the system is
dry, fold down with weight
of water when rain falls.
Other types are manually
operated. *Courtesy of Chapiewsky's, Inc.*

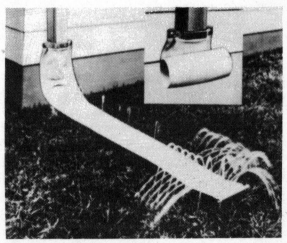

"Rain drains" are available for attaching to bottoms of downspouts to carry water away from foundation walls. Some are
made of flexible plastic, and roll out on lawn when water flows.
Some reroll automatically, other must be rerolled by the home-
owner. *Courtesy of Chapiewsky's, Inc.*

REPAIR AND MAINTENANCE TECHNIQUES

Although some rain-carrier repairs are as simple as painting, there are others which may invite consideration of this question:

Is it better to fix the element involved, or to replace it?

For example, a split downspout can be repaired by some such method as applying fiberglass and sealer over the crack, or riveting on a metal patch. But it's a lot of work, and your time might serve you better if it were spent replacing the downspout, a simple job. On the other hand, a rusted spot in the middle of a long length of gutter might be more efficiently repaired than replaced.

Always keep in mind the simplicity of the system, the relative ease with which elements can be removed and replaced, plus the most important factor of all: Replacement parts with modern pre-finishing techniques will quite likely outlast your repair job.

Peeling paint. All too often, paint starts to come off the rain-carrying system of a house before it fails on the rest of the house. Metal is, or used to be, hard to keep painted, largely because the key to success is proper priming, and priming is often carelessly done. After all, it doesn't show. Today's pre-primed metals and, in fact, today's better-sticking primers, make the job easier and more permanent.

When gutters and downspouts show only here-and-there failure, the best thing to do is repaint the bad areas. Then, if paint starts to peel in other places, you have a pretty good indication that the entire system may need refinishing, sooner or later.

Handle the spots that are peeling this way:

• Use a putty knife or similar tool to peel off *all the paint* that will come loose around the area. Examine the gutter or downspout for several feet on either side, to be sure that there are no bubbles or other indications of failing adhesion. If you find them, scrape away the bad paint.

• When you have scraped away all loose and flaking paint, use medium sandpaper to "feather" the hard edges of the sound paint, so they won't be unsightly when the job is finished.

• If the bare metal shows loose or flaking rust, use a wire brush to remove all that will come off.

• If the bare metal shows no rust, but is instead relatively bright, use a multi-solvent liquid like Wil-Bond or Liquid Sandpaper on a rag to wipe the surface of the metal. The purpose of this step is to remove any substances from the surface that foil good painting and to provide better adhesion.

• Use a specific primer for the first coat, not an ordinary paint. Some modern paints are labeled "self-priming" and give excellent service, ordinarily. However, remember that you are working on what seems to be a problem area. Buy a can of specific primer for that first coat. There are excellent latex-base primers with relatively short drying time, if you want to use one to make the job go faster. Feather out the paint at the edges, to avoid an abrupt line.

• Use either latex house paint or a trim paint in your color for the first coat, feathering it out. If the patch looks all right, you can save the second finish coat until it is time to paint the entire house again, if that day is not too far in the future.

The same fundamentals apply to repainting large areas of the rain-carrier. However, with a lot of scraping, sanding, painting, and ladder moving to do, you might want to investigate the possibility of taking down the gutters. Some systems have eave troughs suspended by means of hangers that "unclip" in one way or another. If it looks easy to take them down, easier than all the ladder work, do it.

Rusted metal. Rust on the outside of gutters and downspouts is always related to failure of finishes, as covered above. If it becomes serious, it is because it was not attended to in a sound preventive maintenance program.

Rust inside the system is different. A fairly serious problem of corrosion may develop in a single season. Repairing it is different, too, since you are interested in protection, not good looks.

Modern rain-carrier materials, among the quality lines, are treated with rust inhibitors both inside and out. The best method of handling rust, therefore, is to maintain these inhibitors: good paint on the outside and a good continuous film on the inside. As you make your semi-annual inspections, watch for indications that the inside of the gutter is starting to go. When you make that discovery, get in there with a brush and a can of paint-on gutter cement. Be sure to bring the coating up the sides of the gutter to the edges.

When you find actual rust, the methods of handling it depend on how bad it is. Can you wirebrush it, then coat it with gutter cement? Or is the rusting so bad that the metal is weakened? If the latter is true, you have three choices: First, you can patch the area with metal and cement. Second, you can replace that part of the gutter which is actually damaged. Third, you can replace the entire element. The methods of doing all three are covered below.

APPLYING A PATCH

• Get hold of a piece of the *same style and size and metal* gutter as that you are repairing, about a foot longer than the area to be patched. Trim the flanged or "hemmed" edges off this material, so that what you end up with is a piece of metal the shape of the gutter. (Actually, you could buy a piece of flashing or other sheet metal and bend it to shape, but it's harder to do.)

• Press the patch into position. It will not fit perfectly, since you are asking its *outside* size to nest *inside* the existing gutter. You will find it simple to make a few minor adjustments in some of the bends and curves so the fit is quite good, however.

• While the patch is in position, drill holes in it for sheet metal screws that will hold it in place, eventually.

• Remove the patch. Lard the area with gutter cement. Put the patch back, and drive the sheet metal screws from the outside on the front and bottom, from the inside on the back.

• End up the job by carefully coating the patch — especially its edges — with cement.

This job is so simple that actually replacing part or all of an element is unnecessary, unless the rust has gone through the metal and no kind of patching would make it look decent.

Important: It is a temptation to use heavy aluminum foil for the patching material. This is okay if you happen to be working on damage to an aluminum system. But, if the system is steel, you may cause corrosion problems (electrolysis) unless you take certain precautions. Make sure that the coating of cement forms a *complete "insulation" between the metals.* Do not use fasteners, but instead bed the foil in a heavy layer of cement, then cover the foil with another layer.

Inserting a new piece of gutter.

• Use a hacksaw or tinsnips to cut out the damaged length of gutter.

• Buy a piece of material about 3″ longer than the piece you cut out.

• Using the techniques shown in the photographs, fit the new piece by slipping it too far into one end, then sliding it back into the other end until the spacing is even at both ends. Use gutter cement and sheet metal screws or pop rivets, as shown.

You may not be able to find a dealer who will sell you less than a 10′ length of material. When that is the case, you will probably discover that at least one end on the new piece will match up with an existing joint and possibly both ends, if your system happens to be built up of 10′ units.

SPLICING GUTTER WITHOUT
A SLIP-ON CONNECTOR

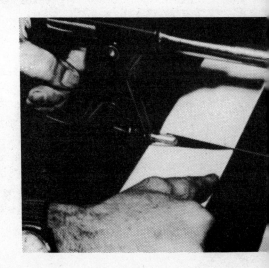

Cut gutter easily with a very fine-tooth hacksaw by working quite flat to the surface and sawing over the far edge of the metal. Rotate the gutter as you finish the cut on each side.

Use square-nose pliers to unbend the hem and the nose on the gutter on one side. Then fit the other piece inside. Use plenty of gutter seal between the two, then fasten with pop rivets or sheet-metal screws. It is best to put fasteners in bottom first, to pull joint tight.

Apply seal to the joint both inside and out. When it is dry, paint the joint to match the rest of the system.

Replacing a unit. This solution is the easiest of all. Take out the screws or drill out the rivets that hold the piece in at both ends. Remove any nails. Put the new length in, using cement and using the same screw and rivet positions with the new fasteners.

THE PROBLEM OF GUTTER HANGERS

When you replace more than a couple of feet of gutter, you are sure to run into one or more hangers, which are usually spaced every 32″ or so. Some hangers wrap around the gutter, some clip around, some fit inside in a manner that makes them demountable. You loosen them, take the gutter down, then refit them around the replacement. On top of this, some installation may have nails through the gutter into the fascia or rafter ends or some other element of the eave construction.

It is not necessary to match the hangers (it may in many cases be impossible) as long as you match their function. Check at your building supply dealer, who will handle several styles, for the one that is easiest for you to use in your situation. As with any element you are replacing, it is a good idea to take a hanger to the lumberyard, show it to the dealer, and let him give you one that will work for you.

CHECKING THE SYSTEM FOR ADEQUATE PITCH

Although it isn't particularly inviting work examining the rain-carrying equipment during a rain, you can come out to the same place by hauling a garden hose up the ladder on a sunny day. Make these checks:

BASIC TYPES OF HANGERS
FOR EAVE TROUGHS

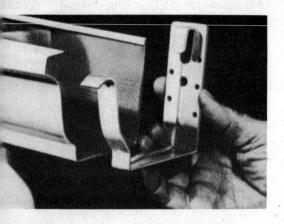

Fascia clip is typical of hangers that fasten to the fascia board at the eaves. If the fascia is not vertical, wedges of the proper angle make this and similar types of mountings effective. A great advantage of the fascia clip is the ease of adjustment up and down on the board for proper pitch.

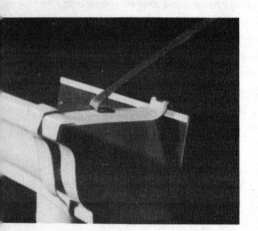 

Strap hanger fastens to the roof itself, and is not dependent on eave design. Properly installed, the strap is under a shingle (raise the flap to nail it), not on top of the roof, as at right.

Easiest kind of hanger to use is the spike and ferrule. The ferrule, actually a metal tube, molds the edges of the gutter and the proper spacing. Spike must go into a solid member, preferably a rafter end.

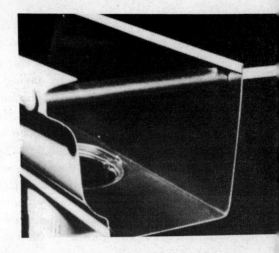

• Let the water from the hose trickle into the gutter at the high end of a run, that is, at the end opposite the downspout outlet. When there is a downspout at both ends of a gutter run, it means that the high spot is, or should be, in the middle. This is the case when a run is much longer than 20′. If it is much longer than about 40′ there may be three downspouts, one at each end, and one in the middle. There will be two high spots, too, half way between the ends and the middle. Not all rain-carrier installations follow this rule, and the result may be overflowing, because the run is so long that the roof sends too much water down for the trough to handle.

• Check for puddling by letting the hose trickle into the gutter until the water has made its way to the downspouts. Remove the hose. Wait until the water movement has stopped, i.e. until it is standing still in the trough. It is simple, then, to watch the water dry. If it leaves stretches where the water stands, you know that the gutter should be raised at those points.

To correct these low spots you must modify the hangers that are involved. Start by laying in the trough a strip of straight-and-true 1 x 2 or 2 x 2 lumber long enough to span the low spot. The sag of the gutter will show beneath this board. It must be raised until the space between board and gutter disappears.

The exact method of doing this will depend on the kind of hangers and the method of installation involved. First, of course, you must remove any nails that occur in the sagging area. Then, you must either raise the hangers or increase their tension, depending on their design. If spike-and-ferrule hangers are used, pull the spikes and redrive them. Some hangers may have slip-joints intended specifically for such adjustment. In some others you may have to twist a wire suspension or crimp one that is a strap of metal. Whichever method your system dictates, use it to pull the gutter up until there is no longer a sag beneath the straightedge. If it is necessary, add new hangers.

It is important in all this that the fasteners at each end of the sag remain in place, to hold firm that part of the gutter which is in proper alignment.

INSTALLING A NEW RUN OF GUTTER

It is by far easier to install a new gutter run than to repair an old one. The steps involved are these:

• Take down the old material carefully enough so that you can assemble it on the ground. On a driveway, walk, or level stretch of lawn is the best place to do it.

• Lay out the new material beside the old, making it exactly the same length, with outlet elements in the same places.

• Join the pieces, using cement and rivets and connectors, as shown in the accompanying photographs. The replacement is now ready to be hoisted into position.

Establishing the pitch. Keep in mind that the ideal pitch is at least ½″ for each 20′ of run and that an inch is better. Here's how to establish the pitch:

STRING

To determine the correct slope for your gutters, tie a chalk line to a nail driven into the fascia board and, using a line level, adjust the line until the bubble is centered. Then lower the line 1″ for a run of 20′, or slightly less than ⅛″ in a 2′ span.

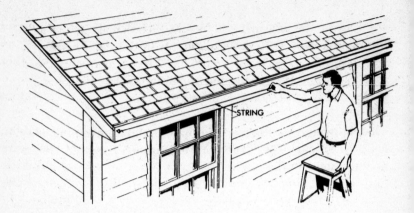

STRING

When the chalk line is secured at the desired slope, pull it out at the center and let it snap, marking a line on the board.

If you replace the gutter spans by yourself, suspend far end first on a circular wire held by a nail, then attach your end along chalk line.

1. Tap on a nail at the high end of the run, as high up on the fascia as convenient. (In some cases there may be no fascia, and the nail will have to go into a rafter end or other element.)

2. Fasten a length of mason's line or other slim but stout cord to the nail.

3. Move to the low end of the run and draw the string tight.

4. Hang a line level (less than a dollar at any hardware store) on the string. Adjust the string up and down until the bubble in the level is properly centered. *Important:* The string must be drawn tight enough so that any sag is negligible.

5. Measure down 1″ from the point where the level is true. Drive another nail.

6. Make the line fast and taut between the two nails.

7. By snapping the line or marking with a pencil, indicate the slope of the gutter along the fascia or other board or boards. This is the line which the edge of the gutter must follow.

Again, the type of fasteners you use must depend on the style of your eaves. But, since you don't have to match up with anything, pick a type of hanger that is easiest to install.

WHEN DOWNSPOUTS CLOG

If you use leaf guards or screens properly, chances are you'll never have trouble with clogging downspouts. Any debris that gets through the guard will be small enough to wash away. But, if you do find that a spout isn't draining:

- Do not try to force the impediment on through with a

If you need to repair roof gutters held by nails and ferrules, pull out the nails with a vise-grip type plier using a twisting motion. Hammer claws will dent the surrounding gutter rails.

broomstick or something similar. That way, you'll only pack it tighter.

• Use a plumber snake, from the top or bottom or both, as a means of digging the impacted debris loose. Combine this operation with a garden hose on full force, so hydraulics help you with the job. (Sometimes the bathroom plunger can move debris in downspouts.)